PRAISE FOR I'D RATH

MW00777137

"Zach Goldberg writes like an inventor. Making the page his playground, his imaginative approaches to craft are thrilling. The writing in *I'd Rather Be Destroyed* is as brilliant as it is easeful. The collection is proof of the healing nature of art, guiding us towards beauty in spite of where we might be convinced it can't be found. Goldberg never leaves the reader lost. Each page is a home we are invited into. Each line is a table we sit down at, grateful."

– Andrea Gibson, *You Better Be Lightning* and *Lord of the Butterflies*

"*I'd Rather Be Destroyed* is an intricate map shepherding its reader into multiple possibilities of home, a collection of poems that unfold and unlock each other. Zach Goldberg shows us, through introspection and formal dexterity, that diaspora can be a nesting doll of ghosts, that correlations and revelations share a piercing proximity. I am in awe of this book, the way its meanings are cleaved to produce deeper resonance; a split-atom I understand even more through its blaze."

– Junious 'Jay' Ward, *Composition*

"Dexterous and innovative in form and far reaching in story and lyricism, Goldberg's collection holds, challenges, and surprises with poems that at once question and reaffirm Jewish identity, exploring its connection to God and Homeland, to family, ancestry, and selfhood. Ebbing between erasures, hermit crabs, contrapuntals, invented forms, and more traditional stanziacs, Goldberg's poems traverse between intimate struggles with addiction to geopolitical conflicts in the Middle East and the vast world between, always grounding the personal, collective, and global in powerful image and deft musicality. "i brace myself to be passed over." we are told in the opening poem, and the rest of the collection moves through us, as though we were a house unmarked by lamb's blood, from the aching present to an aching past and back again, hurt and violence sung and carried. Though not healed, these poems reach towards the possibility of healing, inviting us to keep reaching too, for "Home, the place you leave / to find." Goldberg created a home through these poems. It is a beautiful debut!"

– Julia Kolchinsky Dasbach, *40 Weeks, The Many Names for Mother*, and *Don't Touch the Bones*

I'd Rather Be Destroyed

I'd Rather Be Destroyed

poems by

Zach Goldberg

Button Publishing Inc.
Minneapolis
2024

I'D RATHER BE DESTROYED
POETRY
AUTHOR: Zach Goldberg
COVER ART: Annemarie
COVER DESIGN: Zoe Norvell
AUTHOR PHOTOGRAPHY: Mel Nigro

ALL RIGHTS RESERVED

© 2024 by Zach Goldberg

Published by Button Poetry
Minneapolis, MN 55418 | http://www.buttonpoetry.com

Manufactured in the United States of America
PRINT ISBN: 978-1-63834-200-7
EBOOK ISBN: 978-1-63834-106-2
AUDIOBOOK ISBN: 978-1-63834-105-5

First Printing

TABLE OF CONTENTS

Ninth Plague   1

First Drink   3

Wine / Water / Blood   4

okay, stop me if you've heard this one   6

Punnett Square for the Ways I Die   10

Second Drink   12

Leil Shimurim   13

From Here   14

Barbra's Nose   16

ELEVEN   17

Everything I Want to Hear   21

J.I.N.O. (Jew In Name Only)   22

Incantation   24

A list of rituals to invoke Hypnos the God of Sleep   26

Third Drink   28

The Plane Lands at Ben Gurion and Every Passenger
Bursts Into Song   30

I Grab a Loose Thread and Pull   33

NUREMBERG LAWS   35

Birthright   42

My Depression Explains Me to My Mother   43

my mouth   45

Fourth Drink   46

Twice-Contained   47

Red / Sea   50

Sitting Shiva   52

tradescantia   54

Matryoshka   55

Makot Mitzrayim 56

Fifth Drink 60

What We're Owed 61

The Discovery of Death 62

Tetragrammaton 63

listen, the ghosts out in the old country can't light candles 65

The Other Moses 67

My Shadow and the Bottle 69

Next Year in Jerusalem 72

Notes 75

Acknowledgements 79

About the Author 83

Author Book Recommendations 85

I'd Rather Be Destroyed

NINTH PLAGUE

with a line borrowed from Eduardo C. Corral

i'm an Aries, which means i'd rather be destroyed
than ignored. my mother loves to tell

the story, how as an infant, i once bit down
on her breast when she raised her chin

to chastise my older brother. attention
is my currency of choice, never mind

its proximity to violence. i grew up wanting
a reason to kick. to be kicked. i grew up believing

there's a scientific explanation for everything
that happens in the Bible. pillar of salt.

column of fire. i learned that an act of G-d
can be predicted by the movements

of large bodies, a simple trick of astrophysics.
three days after the solar eclipse, my mother calls

to tell me the Torah scrolls have been moved
from our synagogue to a safe location. this must be

the end of days. i mark the blood over my door.
i brace myself to be passed over. unseen hand

that blots out first the sun and then
each firstborn son. what makes my brother

such a worthy offering? can't i
tempt a destroying angel? can't i

sit on the receiving end of wrath?
tremble if G-d forgets you. tremble

if G-d remembers. darkness was the ninth plague
and then there was violence.

FIRST DRINK

when you're a kid, it's easy to think that having an "addictive personality" means no one can get enough of you. then you grow up, and your poetry professor tells you to stop writing about whiskey because there is absolutely nothing interesting about the fact that you're a drunk. when i first learned about alcohol-induced amnesia, or "blacking out," i was still able to stop myself from it. i spent my nights creating new mixed drinks and good memories. i can't ever forget the first time i had just the right amount, and it didn't have to be alcohol. it could've been anything. it can be an addiction before it is ever a vice. because if i swallowed it and finished it and it didn't kill me, it must be some kind of medicine, the first thing worth my good health. i'm not remembering it perfectly, but there is a trap door beneath my feet that no one has the key to. i can't open it, not even with a drink, not even when i offer to give up my entire body. but all the same, praise to the bottle sunrise. praise the best friend therapist, so designated by this holy mixture. praise the Lyft driver, this unlucky ferryman crossing the river Styx. poor old god. when i am unable to make the passage, he does it for me.

WINE / WATER / BLOOD

WINE

wine was the first miracle
of Jesus which must mean
something about G-d
His penchant for spectacle
tonight consider the empty glass
one prophet can transubstantiate
into a brimming celebration
the length of a country
liquor too can be a consecration
so it became the way i practiced
a righteous justification from the
bottle i thought i'd be
a drop in the bucket of
history the most tragic martyr
devotion debauchery
the line between them is blurry
a sinner feigning sainthood
without knowing the cost

WATER

i was conjured in a temple but
like water pulled from a stone it
should never have happened
prophets always seem to float
instead of sinking once again
the drinking water magicked
another prophet opens a river
where a country ought to be
we rationalize what we can
worshipping the past i learned
Biblical stories of near-drowning
Noah on the edge of the flood the
messenger's messy work
arrives natural as the water
my lone cup runneth over with
no i don't think myself a prophet
i'm a different figure altogether
remember how this all started

BLOOD

no it wasn't the blood
soured in our own hands
it wasn't Moses his staff raised
above G-d's wretched work
the enemy's prayer fouled
by divine intervention transformed
into a festering wound
no it wasn't the circular way
i was taught to inherit suffering
to handle pain like
using a knife to open a
knife our intimacy with ruin is
older than prophecy older than
sacrifice a tangle of
blood and brotherhood but
it's much simpler than that just
Cain preparing to kill
with a stone

OKAY, STOP ME IF YOU'VE HEARD THIS ONE

so a minister, a Jew, and an atheist walk into a bar
and the bartender says "what'll you have?"
...and they order a scotch!

get it?

the joke is
that all three of them are the same person:

my father!

he is an atheist Jewish minister.
and he always orders a scotch.

okay, stop me if you've heard this one:

so my father walks into a synagogue.
he does not know any of the Hebrew prayers
but he knows all their beautiful names.
he knows the rabbi must bless the wine
before he is permitted to drink it.
however, my father is the type of atheist
who will shake a holy man's hand
with his fingers crossed behind his back.
so naturally, he becomes an ordained minister
(online)
like a joke no one but him finds funny.

stop me if you've heard this one:

so my father walks into a bar.
he does not know the name

of anything he would not drink,
so he asks the bartender for any drink with a beautiful name.

so my father walks into a bar
and sees a holy man at the counter
the bartender says "what'll you have?"
and my father asks for absolution
with his fingers crossed behind his back,
and he is not sure who he is speaking to.

so my father walks out of AA
because they mention G-d one too many times
and he is his own higher power.

so my father walks into a bar and never leaves.

so i walk into a bar
and see my father at the counter.
i ask him what he's doing *here*
in my joke, and he says
"can you even imagine a bar without me in it?"

so my father and i walk into a bar together
and the bartender says grace.

my father and i walk into a bar
and the bartender says "what'll you have?"
and my father orders a scotch
                    and i order a scotch
                              and we become our
                    own fathers.

so i walk into a bar
and there's a rabbi at the counter.
the bartender says "what'll you have?" and i say
"make me something with a beautiful name.

i don't much care what's in it."
and the rabbi says
"shining one."   "morning star."
"even G-d has beautiful names   for the devil."

so i walk into my parents' house
and my mother has hidden all the wine bottles.
i walk into AA with my fingers crossed behind my back.
i walk into bars again and again.
i have nights that don't end when the night ends.
i tell jokes no one but me finds funny.

stop me if you've heard this one:

so i walk into a bar
and the bartender says "what'll you have?"
and "i say i don't know
what did you serve my father?"

and the bartender says
"actually i haven't seen him around much lately."
and i know my father didn't get religious
but maybe he did find absolution
and it wasn't at the bottom of a bottle.
maybe he swallowed the same curse so many times
that it turned into a prayer in his mouth
and so my father (minister. Jew. atheist. addict.)
walks into grace as though it were a bar
        or a synagogue
some room he does not belong in
but finds himself in anyway.

and i order a scotch

and then it's just me   at a bar   drinking his drink
        telling his joke   and no one is laughing.

stop me if you've heard this one.

no really stop me
if you've heard it.

somebody stop me.

PUNNETT SQUARE FOR THE WAYS I DIE

	FATHER	
%		**Dominant**
MOTHER **Dominant**		i entered the world through a red gate pried open by pure chance. in this case, a Monday in spring. in this case, both parents on their knees working the strip of earth by the front walkway they like to call a "garden." caging blueberries to defend them from the birds, each metal wire as sharp as a whistle. as sharp as blood. when two jazz musicians fall in love, it's called a ballad. when they laugh, it's called a standard. when they have a son, it's called a dirge. my parents are still in love. that is their most impressive trait.
Recessive		here, a country of probability. here, an alternate universe where i am no longer afraid. if i had arrived here, i would still be sick, just a different kind. golden light through the window and i sneeze in flocks of starlings. mom touts the cobalt of my irises. dad lets me try a sip of whiskey. here, i don't look like what i am, what's hidden in the shadow of every joke. this is how i learned to hate crowds and crave attention at the same time. i can't fall back asleep after 7am. i don't smoke, but i'll take a cigarette if you've got it.

FATHER

Recessive	
i'm the only twelve-year-old on the ellipticals at the JCC. mom has to stop and have a full conversation with every adult we run into. i don't have the patience to be a child, and i'm too selfish to be a parent. the afternoon dad's flight lands is the last time i don't know his blood type. room of a thousand hands. mom's frantic yelling at the woman at the intake counter. dad's absolute and mortal guilt. i was raised here but didn't know it until years later. from the hospital bed, i see death but cannot gauge its distance.	**Dominant**
i sang the songs. i ate the meals. i opened every door. i walked through every possibility. they say the gene for hair loss is maternal, but based on everything i've seen, heredity is just a myth. my parents live each day with the knowledge of their own weakness passed down to me. when i inherit something from them, they do not in turn relinquish it. they give me a thing they still own, a cutting of their grief. i have to believe that more than one thing can be true at the same time. it's the only way i get out of here alive.	**Recessive**

MOTHER

SECOND DRINK

when you 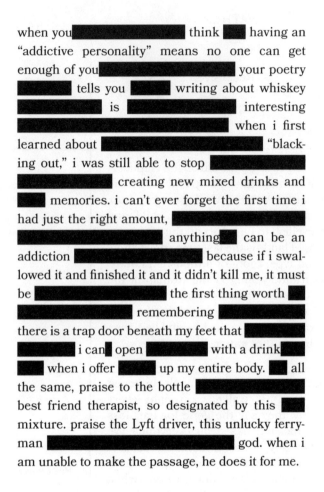 think ▮ having an
"addictive personality" means no one can get
enough of you███████████████ your poetry
██████ tells you ████ writing about whiskey
██████████ is ████████████████ interesting
██████████████████████████ when i first
learned about ██████████████████ "black-
ing out," i was still able to stop ████████████
████████████ creating new mixed drinks and
███ memories. i can't ever forget the first time i
had just the right amount, ███████████████
████████████████████ anything██ can be an
addiction ████████████ because if i swal-
lowed it and finished it and it didn't kill me, it must
be █████████████ the first thing worth ██
██████████ remembering ████████████
there is a trap door beneath my feet that ████████
██████ i can█ open ███████ with a drink███
███ when i offer ████ up my entire body. ██ all
the same, praise to the bottle ████████████
best friend therapist, so designated by this ██
mixture. praise the Lyft driver, this unlucky ferry-
man ████████████████████ god. when i
am unable to make the passage, he does it for me.

LEIL SHIMURIM

my father used to fall asleep on the couch
before the seder ended. he was probably
tired of hearing the same long story
we told every year. "what makes this night
different from all other nights?" miracle
night. joyous night. night of vigils. night of cups.
we leave the door open and wait for revelation:
Elijah slipping silent through the portal
to drink his fill. i've seen my father pour
the prophet's glass but never seen it emptied.
yet somehow, it's always gone by the end
of the night. did i miss the arrival? the announcement?
we wait and we wait. red glass of wine.
red drop of blood. when we beckon Elijah
to the table, we are asking for the promise
of a savior. the moshiach. the rapture
disappearing in a glass. while we celebrate,
our fingers stain from the work. red night.
guarded night. vicious night of corpses.
our rejoicing shakes the world, but my father
always knew this night was closely watched
so he learned to relax. he fell asleep
on the couch, and we wondered at the missing
glass of wine. where did it go if not
to the heavens? the door was open
but no one saw the visitor step through it.
in retrospect, we all knew, but no one
dared to question. there's only one man
who understood that a glass of wine
is an end in itself. an invitation to vanish.
we should've expected it: my father.

FROM HERE

my folks ain't from here. that's what i'd say
whenever asked why my accent doesn't
drip molasses thick, why vinegar and pork fat
are absent from my parents' kitchen.

i never asked them why my accent isn't
like theirs either - we're all transplants,
all absent from our parents' kitchens
and mothertongues. i played southern once,

like them, but either we all translate
the synagogue song or America severs
our mothertongues. i played southern one
summer, spit bluegrass, wished i could forget

the synagogue songs. America never was.
it's a myth. years after my parents' last road trip
summer (split gas, blues) i bet they can't forget
the drive south. their thread unspools like

a myth in the years since their last road trip.
there's a science to it, knowing how
far south to drive until a threat unspools from
a question: *are you from New York? are you a Jew?*

there's a silence to it, not knowing which
history will silhouette the evening. once more,
the question: *are you a Jew? are you from New York?*
yes. see how we speak? how we sit

in history's silhouette? this evening, one more
promised land lies through its teeth,
and i see how it speaks. how it spits.
how we don't belong, yet everywhere we've lived

a promised land lies. through its teeth,
a shrill voice that sounds of home. what can i say?
i don't belong anywhere i've ever lived.
in Minnesota or California or North Carolina

if my shrill voice sounded of home, what would i say?
i'm from thick dripped molasses, vinegar and pork fat,
from Brooklyn and Russia and the countries before.
but my folks aren't from here. that's what i'd say.

BARBRA'S NOSE

o, sparrow prow.
crooked claw.
o, funny girl
on the funny girl's face.
the first time i saw you, holy
weapon unsheathed from beneath
Fanny Brice's leopard print collar,
(*hello, gorgeous*) i recognized you
immediately from my grandmother's
knowing smile. her Brooklyn accent.
my mother's soprano. o, yiddish beak
adorning the jewbird. kosher canvas sail
that caught the wind. i heard when Babs
got into showbiz they wanted to rub you out,
to straighten that devious deviated septum
into more gentle and gentile contours.
sideways crown. unmuzzled animal. the inventor
of the modern rhinoplasty was a German Jew
named Jacques Joseph. he knew folks would pay
through the nose for the cut. the newest craze, a chance
for admittance to the country club. you're an old story:
the same hooked bill that killed christ, cracked G-d dead.
and yes, maybe a cousin or two complied, tried to disappear
their Jew, but no nosejob can unknow its own mug. Barbra sliced
a letter from the center of her name rather than part with you.
o, clipped wing above her top lip that can peck, sniff, but never got
snipped off a cliff's edge or a knife's tip. o, mountain on the side
of a mountain. my mother sings in the shape of you. celestial
wedge that catches the light, all glamor and suffering
and music. a temple built out of insults.
mast of a ship going somewhere
they can't follow.

ELEVEN

after Patricia Smith

1.
you cut your rattail off. you've been growing it
since preschool. back then, you used to thread it with
turquoise beads and drape it over your shoulder,
but something's changed this year. maybe you hate how
kids in line behind you pull it then pretend
like nothing's happened, or maybe you're starting
middle school soon and don't want to be different
in a way you don't understand. before she
snips it off, mom braids it with three strands. after,
she puts it in an envelope and keeps it
in her dresser. just like that, the split ending.

2.
on Thursdays, Maggie's dad picks you up after
school, and you sit facing her in the jump seats
of his dirty blue pickup truck while he drives
downtown to drop you both off at the local
arts council where you learn to live truthfully
under imaginary circumstances.
the spring production is some Arthurian
legend, and during tech week, all your castmates
dare the two of you to kiss backstage. her breath
on your cheek in the dark. the almost of it.
the pale awe. you pull back at the last second.

3.
you don't say much, sitting in the family
therapist's dusty office. you fidget with
an Etch A Sketch. your brother does the talking
here. a few days ago, you watched him leap from
the high-dive. while plummeting, he swerved mid-fall
to avoid landing on another boy and

hit the concrete. you gawk at the size of his
cast. his bruises. here, he's the star each week. he's
in the reticle. most days, you're just trying
to avoid his aim, but now you know his truth:
there is, somewhere, a seed of mercy in him.

4.
your bunkmates at summer camp introduce you
to the word *fuck* as in *fuck yea* or *fuck you*
though at this point it means so little about
what lives in the world. rather, language becomes
a test, the ropes course upon which you prove your
manhood. you collect the word and harness its
dangerous magic. shout *fuck* and the world snaps
to attention. everything is *so fucking*
awesome. you want the word without its damage,
lust but not its purpose. its magnetic pull.
you *don't give a fuck.* that's your right as a child.

5.
you sprain your wrist when five or six boys push you
off your bike and jump you on the path behind
the baseball field. you know you're not supposed to
be here, city where *y'alls* and *ain'ts* surge from your
mouth to circle like a cloud of moths around
some backyard porch light's false moon. you swear this town
is nothing but the heat shimmer on the back
of a church grandma's neck. cicadas as they make
the sky into a rainstick tipping over.
heat lightning nights. your wrist bound in athletic
tape. a place you know you're not supposed to be.

6.
on the first day of band class, Mr. Guptill
puts the horns out on display like merchandise.
you choose the trumpet for its glamor, how it
shimmers in your hands. imagine the brass a

second throat. third arm. organ somewhere between
fingertips and the air above your mother's
voice. despite this, the intricacies of breath
and memory are new to you. can't form a
firm embouchure for your life. you walk around
and buzz your lips on the mouthpiece, its weight like
a silent pebble held between two fingers.

7.
you flick the zipper on your trapper-keeper
back and forth like a light switch as you stand in
line for a flu shot behind the other sixth
graders. Ms. Ford watches you take the needle.
"that wasn't so bad now, was it?" was it? you
stand, and the blood swells beneath you. sudden bell
in the marrow. the air crackles, subdivides
each word on approach. you wake on the cold floor
and don't know which is worse: the embarrassment
or the fear. no one told you – the remedy
for sickness is another kind of sickness.

8.
the year tugs you in a direction you're not
sure you want to go. you still write stories full
of dragons and ancient prophecies, still want
to make believe, to turn a tree branch into
a sword. your friends want to play pickup ball at
Seth's house, though you know everytime you miss and
the ball rolls down the driveway, you'll be the one
responsible for running into the street
to retrieve it – not the kind of adventure
you had in mind. you're not so accurate with
those kinds of games, so you stick to pretending.

9.
you've never heard of lymph nodes, so you study
the pattern in the upholstery on the couch

while dad explains the science, tells you the odds
of survival. the nape of his neck goes bald
first, and the rest soon follows - eyebrows and all
(though he didn't have much hair to begin with).
his truck still smells like Marlboros, even on
the days he comes home too tired to talk, too
tired to crack his jokes. he falls asleep watching
The Sopranos, and while he snores, you apply
a temporary rose tattoo on his scalp.

10.
one night when Jake is sleeping over, you sneak
into the den and surf HBO for porn.
you chatter with anticipation, but soon
dull stars of areolas slip in and out
of frame, and you both fall silent with mythic
understanding. you don't look at eachother
for fear of what might pass between you. instead,
you hold yourselves separately and quietly
until you're satisfied with the little you
know of desire. the small fact of the bright screen
becomes the root of a secret. becomes shame.

11.
you're almost twelve now, sitting in Hebrew school
twice a week, where lately all talk is of your
final year of childhood, the prayers that will make
you a man. the words come simply enough, but
the melodies are unfamiliar. you must
learn new symbols, the diacritical marks
that hang above each line of litany to
instruct you on its tune. look up and read the
music. you stand on the precipice, looking
through the door to other doors. there is language
above language. there are marks that point the way.

EVERYTHING I WANT TO HEAR

Tell me you had a rock collection
and hunted crayfish in streams.
Tell me you skipped stones. You
shot air rifles at squirrels and
picked your nose. Say you told
ghost stories and believed them.
You fought. You fell in love with girls
who didn't love you back. Say you lost
the house keys and broke in
through the back window or that
you broke in through the back window
anyway. Say you swam naked across
the lake. Say you never lit a match
on the first try. Say you burned
insects to watch their funeral pyres.
You were cruel or you were curious.
You weren't sure which you were more of.
Say you pretended to play guitar
until you could. You loved your dog.
You discovered the satisfaction
of rare meat. You lowered the hoop
on your basketball court. You drank
milk past its expiration date. Say
you invented new ways to defeat yourself.

J.I.N.O. (JEW IN NAME ONLY)

after Jon Sands and Angel Nafis

J.I.N.O. forgot what his Hebrew name means.
J.I.N.O. knows the name, just not what it means.
J.I.N.O. cinnamon raisin bagel with strawberry cream cheese.
J.I.N.O. one shankbone shy of a full seder plate.
one oil lamp short of a hanukiah.
J.I.N.O. circumcised. does that not count anymore?
J.I.N.O. only 2nd grade Hebrew reading level but
J.I.N.O. still bar mitzvahed. still had the party.
J.I.N.O. majored in religious studies, just not Judaism.
J.I.N.O. at the church. at the mosque. at the monastery.
J.I.N.O. at his best friend's house on Christmas morning.
J.I.N.O. at Biscuitville on Yom Kippur
bacon-egg-and-cheese before services.
J.I.N.O. treif by 10am. at synagogue
J.I.N.O. memorized all the blessings but not what they mean.
but still, he memorized them, didn't he?
wanted to sing the harmony like his mother.
J.I.N.O. won't spell G-d. can't say יְהֹוָה
J.I.N.O. on birthright, making out with another
J.I.N.O. in the back of the bus. at the dive bar in Tel Aviv.
J.I.N.O. spent his childhood dumping spare change
into those little blue Jewish National Fund tzedakah boxes
J.I.N.O. can draw the 1967 borders with his eyes closed.
J.I.N.O. memorizes things, just not what they mean.
J.I.N.O. understands guilt.
J.I.N.O. sits beside guilt at services,
J.I.N.O. split down the middle like the Red Sea.
J.I.N.O. knows the blessings. can still recite
his haftorah portion. can still see the bullet holes blooming
around the windows of a temple in the Galilee.
memorized his mother's song floating

through the vaulted rafters of a synagogue
and one of these things must make him Jewish.
must be the reason he knows guilt
and prays in a language he doesn't understand
to a god with a name no one can say.

INCANTATION

If I know anything about you
(and I do) it's that you didn't lose faith
until the first time you entered a church.
This says more about your sense of humor
than your skepticism, that your name means Rock
though you move like water. I wonder
would you say G-d is benign
in the way a tumor is?

You know better than most of us
that we don't get all our words from books
or bodies. Good religion comes to us
when we need it most, even if we don't recognize it
(and we don't). Repetition is the key
to any successful ritual. It could be the mantra
I repeat every morning on my cushion.
The prayer poised on my tongue
as I drove you to the emergency room.

Prayer, which is nothing but the rope
that pulls a boat in for docking. It doesn't
make exceptions one way or the other,
not even for heretics. That day at the hospital
it made itself a knot around your bed.
It held against the current of the IV drip.
You can tell both where a liquid is going
and where it comes from. Maybe that's why
years later, I followed you down the river.
You are a tradition. You were and are still
practiced. You are practicing.

Dear father, where do you think I went
for those fifteen seconds? Where were you?
This is to say, though you never put your hands

together, never said the words, still
I am here. Like you, every bit a skeptic,
but if I've learned one thing from religion
(and I have), it's that you can conjure
the memory of a man into the world
merely by repeating his name.

A LIST OF RITUALS TO INVOKE HYPNOS, THE GOD OF SLEEP

before anything else, you can simply breathe.
Hypnos, the god of Sleep is summoned
first and foremost by the sound of the human breath.
the rhythmic rise and fall of your chest
is a conjuring in and of itself. you can
abstain from cannabis. from coffee.
you can run three miles a day and drink
nothing but water. light incense
and let it burn while you fester in your sheets.
(everything puts you to sleep eventually.)
you can brew a tea from the roots of a poppy.
unspool the sweater your mother knit
and with its wool, weave a new blanket
the exact weight and shape of your lover's arms.
proper worship demands sacrifice.
what are you least willing to give up? break it
with your own dreamless teeth.
it's no coincidence, that insomnia mimics prayer.
the repetition. the desperation. the obsession
with voice regardless of its efficacy.
everyone knows that Hypnos, the God of Sleep
is the son of Nyx the Night and Erebus the Darkness.
with this in mind, you can welcome
any shadow that crosses your threshold.
feed it and He may mistake it for family.
barring that, your options are limited.
you can renounce light. you can shatter
every bright bulb in the city. you can
return to the same bar every night to greet
your friends with their long slender necks.
their citrus perfume and liver ridicule.
the ritual weight of a glass bottle tipping over.
it may work for a while, but ultimately

if He won't be seduced by honey or vinegar
the only option left is fire.
there are no halfway martyrs here,
only more potent prayers,
new sacraments with names dreamt up
in white rooms. trazodone. hydroxyzine.
lorazepam. these small and brooding knots
slipped on the tongue. and though you may fear
the rings of benzene, no weapon
formed against this bond will wake you.
dreamer's eucharist. nightmare covenant.
inside this tiny disk you can lose yourself in worship.
become so devoted to the practice
that you forget the god. here
the altar, and here, the lamb to slaughter.
your mind, a single-hymned choir. and at last
He comes. He conjures. He magics the night.
and you will know His presence like a miracle
in reverse. you and your fouled holy water.
your insignificant offerings.
you will learn that there are no sacrifices
you can make that would give you any kind of rest
you'd want to have, but nevertheless
the god comes, stretching your mind
over your body until it is a film so thin
you can see through it, see into the cave
where he lives - Hypnos, the God of Sleep.
And he will smile, his teeth white and cratered
as a wicked moon. and they shine so bright
they blind you. a flicker. a flare. a flash
that might just put you down for good.

THIRD DRINK

"addictive personality" means no one can get
enough ███████████████████
████████████████████ whiskey
███████████████████████
████████████████ when i ███
████████████████ "black-
███ out," i ████████ stop ████████
████████ creating new ████████
███ memories. i can't ███ forget ████
████████████████████████
████████████████████████
████████████ because ██ i ███
████████████ didn't ████████
████████████ first ████████
████████ remember ████████
the ████ trap door ████████████
████████ can █ open ████████ with a drink, ███
███ when i offer ████ up ████████
████ praise to the bottle ████████
best friend the ████ designated ████████
████████ driver, this ████ ferry-
man ████████████████ god. when i
am unable to ████████ he does it for me.

THE PLANE LANDS AT BEN GURION AND EVERY PASSENGER BURSTS INTO SONG

what if i told you i was older than my own homeland? who else can say that? nobody but us

that's exactly what i came for.   your beauty.   liquor talk.   all shit

it's not the type of celebration i was expecting, but this will have to do. the most holy city in

a Jew looks towards Zion, is lost. city where tears flow like rain. country at the grave of hope

knows what it's like to be hunted. we were either murdered or kicked out of every country in

and sugar.   i might never come down.   down.   come down. it took too long

the world and all i can think about is lips. pressurized walls of desire. i make a new prayer

wall our eyes over the destruction. ancient city where waters swell with lost fathers, city on

Europe. that's why you have this opportunity. don't dismiss it. it's the only place in the world

to get this   ground.   don't run. you can't   beat it.   pitch black,

out of wanting what i cannot have. which is more enticing: a lover or a language? a nation or

barren highways, humbled gates and ruins. Jerusalem still cries. lost daughter. drops of

where we truly belong. nowhere else is safe, and Jewish blood is not cheap. not anymore.

full scope, pull it.   whoa. that's a whole lot   of never.   run.

the land on which it lies? look: the longing is a gown. a wicked country of open mouths

blood still fall. return the nation. the lands. the city. the peace. o G-d, my people–

31

NOTES:

Soprano (Line 1) is to be sung in the voice of the poet's grandmother.

Alto (Line 2) is to be sung to the tune of "Come Down" written by Anderson .Paak and Hi-Tek

Tenor (Line 3) is to be sung in the voice of the poet.

Bass (Line 4) is to be sung to the tune of "Hatikvah," the Israeli national anthem composed by Naftali Herz Imber and Samuel Cohen

I GRAB A LOOSE THREAD AND PULL

we yelled ourselves hoarse waiting
for the storm to hit. i wanted it
to be like a movie: you can't really love someone
until you go through a disaster with them.

the day the rain came down
we spent six hours in the living room.
i progressively shed each narrative cliché
until every character abandoned

their primary motive in favor of
Cool Ranch Doritos. it was beautiful.
after the drugs wore off we watched a movie.
later that evening, a friend and i sat

on the steps of someone else's house
and shared a beer. i said i spend
so much time drinking that i no longer know
what effect it has on my emotional state.

she said alcohol doesn't make me feel drunk,
it just makes me feel better. i wanted to hug her
but instead i finished the beer.
the next day i got coffee with someone

i hadn't seen since September.
we sat on a couch. i told her all about
the hurricane, and she listened and smiled
and smelled like she always used to.

i didn't sleep that night. she texted me
as i lay awake in bed, and i could tell
that if we had been speaking
she would've been looking away.

don't be surprised, i responded. i used to be
so afraid of my sweet tooth that it was unhealthy.
destruction is just an appeal to the audience.
that's when it happens:

the clichés flood back through the windows.
the evening rips at the seams
and i imagine threading a needle
back through all the little star-specs.

NUREMBERG LAWS

I. N   E   WS

my name was a martyr's before it was mine.
when called, i am the dead man turning over
on a tongue, his letters realigned inside my grandmother's
language. she told me never to trust anything
that seems too good to be true. that way
when the bad news arrives, it won't feel like news.
will feel like history. all of us prophets – to name
ourselves after the worst before the worst names us.
to preempt the fire before it breaks into our houses.
she taught herself English by playing Scrabble,
so she owns no letters of her own. she borrowed them
from someone who needed them more:
ghosts and those who are not yet ghosts.
people of the coming flames. citizens of ember.

II.   LAWS

Citizenship Law of September 15, 1935

The Reichstag has unanimously enacted the following law, which is promulgated herewith:

Article 1

1. A subject of the state is a person who enjoys the protection of the German Reich and who in consequence has specific obligations toward it.

2. The status of subject of the state is acquired in accordance with the provisions of the Reich and the Reich Citizenship Law.

Article 2

1. A Reich citizen is a subject of the state who is of German or related blood. and proves by his conduct that he is willing and fit to faithfully serve the German people and Reich.

2. Reich citizenship is acquired through the granting of a Reich citizenship certificate.

3. The Reich citizen is the sole bearer of full political rights in accordance with the law.

Article 3

The Reich Minister of the Interior, in coordination with the Deputy of the Führer. will issue the legal and administrative orders required to implement and complete this law.

Law for the Protection of German Blood and German Honor of September 15, 1935

Moved by the understanding that purity of German blood is the essential condition for the continued existence of the German people, and inspired by the inflexible determination to ensure the existence of the German nation for all time, the Reichstag has unanimously adopted the following law, which is promulgated herewith:

Article 1

1. Marriages between Jews and citizens of German or related blood are forbidden. Marriages nevertheless concluded are invalid, even if concluded abroad to circumvent this law.

2. Annulment proceedings can be initiated only by the state prosecutor.

Article 2

Extramarital relations between Jews and citizens of German or related blood are forbidden.

Article 3

Jews may not employ in their households female subjects of the state of German or related blood who are under 45 years old.

Article 4

1. Jews are forbidden to fly the Reich or national flag or display Reich colors.

2. They are, on the other hand, permitted to display the Jewish flag. The exercise of this right is protected by the state.

Article 5

1. Any person who violates the prohibition under Article 1 will be punished with a prison sentence with hard labor.

2. A male who violates the prohibition under Article 2 will be punished with a jail term or a prison sentence with hard labor.

3. Any person violating the provisions under Articles 3 or 4 will be punished with a jail term of up to one year and a fine, or with one or the other of these penalties.

Article 6

The Reich Minister of the Interior, in coordination with the Deputy of the Führer and the Reich Minister of Justice, will issue the legal and administrative regulations required to implement and complete this law.

Article 7

The law takes effect on the day following promulgation, except for Article 3. which goes into force on January 1, 1936.

III.   EMBER

a flag is any prison with one law:
don't look beyond its bars. you don't belong
to any country, although when they draw
the borders you're inside them. you're the wrong
variety of citizen. your name
is in a foreign tongue. they stacked and lit
your language, made a small and meager flame
of sentences. the ash, a grammar spit
onto the soil. when a word ignites
it turns into a star, a lonely point
of light. remember how you wore the bright
insignias? that amber blaze anoints
you all, and so a constellation sung
then breathed a spark into war's ember lung.

IV. NU   MBER   S

war's ember lung
rumbles, grew an
urge: men. brawls.
gun-warm rebels.
we sung rambler
ere, wrung balms,
slung warm beer.
bugler warns me:
realms brew gun-
barrel news, gum
war's numb leger
law, reg. numbers
burn arms. we leg-
blurs. we german?

V. U MBER

We German / as a war / a wall / a quick border-
crossing / Your quartile of grandparents / Your quo-
rum for prayer / Is your blood a minyan? / A warm
red ratio? / Show me your shadow / if it has the
right skull / Can the battered bottoms of your feet
turn sinister? / Can fear cut a path clear across a
country? / Can someone's god break an ocean in
two? / If so, which one? / Which ocean? / Which
god? / Are the tides coming in or going out this eve-
ning? / Will there be a war tomorrow? / When the
sirens come, where can we hide? / Where is a cor-
ner where the light doesn't reach? / And where is a
homeland if not in the dark? / Where did we go
wrong? / How did we do this? / What was your
name when you came here first? / Did it spark? /
Did it sputter? / Did it float off your tongue? / How
do you read a backwards blessing? / How do you
right an upturned ship? / How do you say an unsay-
able word? / And how do you pray? / And how do
you pray? / And how do you pray? / And how do you
/ pray?

VI.   RE   BE   L

and how did you pray in that August morning
before you flared luminous? a death for a cause.
who here would follow all wrong laws to the gallows?
the enemy's language with you in its jaws.

a people untempled. a city unconquered.
unhistoried men with their unslumbered spears.
the streets running red with many a namesake
until the stars come out. i wish you could hear

Baba's perfect English, the pride she felt
when explaining to me how her father read
in three languages, left stones at your gravesite.
someone must stay alive to re-sow the dead.

names will stay dormant as long as they need to.
it's all heat and pressure. gravity. time.
what men from the past can we rob for their letters?
my name was a martyr's before it was mine.

BIRTHRIGHT

have you seen a map of Israel? symphony of cease-
fire lines. disengagement zones. borders that ebb
and rise like the banks of the Galilee. overflow onto
our neighbor's land. we learned from the imperial-
ists: your home means nothing without a Mandate
and a rifle. if you keep watching here you'll start to
see the West Bank barrier. we built the wall beyond
the border. that way we can settle in the gray area
without fear of retribution. it's nice when we get to
be the guards at the checkpoints for once. after all,
we have broken out of enough cages to know how to
build a good one ourselves. up ahead you'll see the
Old City of Jerusalem. call it annexed. call it occu-
pied. it is your inheritance, and that's why we call
this Birthright. it's not as catchy to say biblical guilt
trip. ancestral gaslighting. this bus ride is about
more than a bottle of Dead Sea sand you can take
home to show your parents. you diaspora Jews, as if
your namesakes didn't die in Poland, weren't bur-
ied in congregations. i've seen this country climb
from a graveyard of its own dead names and you're
afraid to leave a few more bodies on the road? what
have they been teaching you about ghosts in Amer-
ica? what have they been telling you about your own
home? that somebody else used to live here? you
think this is a haunted house? you think a Ouija
board ever spelled out PALESTINE? go ahead.
turn off the lights and say "Gaza" three times in a
mirror. see if any spirit comes back to haunt you. by
the time your plane landed here you were already
complicit. so here is a bottle of sand from the Dead
Sea. here is a prayer for safe passage. here is a map
of Israel. now point to it. show me where you live.

MY DEPRESSION EXPLAINS ME TO MY MOTHER

after RJ Walker
after Sabrina Benaim

this isn't ever easy, Susan, but
(can i call you Susan?)
i've been meaning to reach out.
we need to talk about your boy.
your son. don't worry, he's not in trouble
at least not that kind of trouble
though i wonder if the past year
has cracked the fine shell of him.
you and i, we haven't
met before, and though
he may have spoken of me
i'm sure he was not generous.
believe me, we are good friends.
he calls me chemical
imbalance, but you can just say cognitive
record skip. caesura in the grey matter.
i'm here to warn you. your boy is
(how do i say this?)
Susan, your son answers every question
with a question. he gets nervous whenever
he's in a room with only one other person.
if he tells you the truth, it was a mistake,
a magic trick for an audience of one,
an escape of miniscule proportions.
i've tried to negotiate, to be a friend to him
but the concept does not translate. Susan,
he forgot dancefloors. he no longer believes
in windows. i wanted so hard
to make this easy, held him close as a small
bird in my chloroform hands. my gentle
gentle knives. but your boy, your son
(sorry, what was his name?)

he tries to exit through each lapse
in conversation. he grinds his teeth
in his dreams and he never dreams.
not much is where he once was,
just a dull wet spot. just a rag of a boy.
there was a time he thought to bind me
with a chain of hydrocarbons. tried to sweep
me out in a flood of synthetic serotonin.
but i am not so easily replaced. you know
as well as i do that there's no substitute
for a mother's love. and is it true
he barely calls you anymore?
Susan, do you remember the calls?
3am from someone else's bathroom tile?
needlesick in the emergency room?
how are you sure that was your son
and not me? after all, i am with him
most days. he carries me around
like a stone at the bottom of a lake.
like a crow on fire. sometimes
he opens his mouth and i snap
his lover at the neck. what a rush
to be in his throat each morning
and watch from his coffin each night.
we're so bloodclose i think
he's convinced we are family
so i'm reaching out to tell you.
we need to talk, Susan,
he calls me mother now.

MY MOUTH

after Aziza Barnes

red void
around which light is seen.
worry engine windmilling
funerals. wet fortune.
colony of skin. colony
of sharp ants. colony.
rope ladder fire escape to
everything my parents wished for
and everything my grandparents feared.
terrifying ear canal progenitor.
a hand with no bones in it.
where can i put all these night terrors?
in a soft casket? give them a clever autopsy?
a sweet, sweet hospice? the many keys
of a mortal organ. my teeth will thieve
the Pleiades of their bloodline
and walk the sharp shape sound makes
when it leaks from an IV drip. this is it:
my skeleton's best chance
at being taken seriously.

FOURTH DRINK

addictive ▓▓▓ means ▓▓▓

▓▓▓

▓▓▓

when ▓▓▓

i ▓▓▓

can't ▓▓▓

open ▓▓▓ a drink, ▓
i offer ▓▓▓
praise to the bottle ▓▓▓
best ▓ end the ▓▓ designated ▓▓
driver ▓ is ▓▓
god. ▓ i
am unable ▓▓▓ he does it for me.

TWICE-CONTAINED

and just like that
another nation encircles me.
i am twice-contained.
a venn diagram of flags.
your torch and tablet,
two weapons of statehood.
your crown, a bastard halo. i am
a barnacle on your blue-green hull.
explain again how i parasited
my host-home into this abundance.
how i am blamed for the rats
when the rats cannot be found.
my grandparents' parents doubled
their prayers on the crest of migration.
each year, the border of Russia
crossed their cemeteries like a harvest
blade. each synagogue, an illuminated
waiting room for the twice-promised voyage.
they couldn't be picky with so few choices
so when you said come, they came. beckoned
by thick shoals at the bottom of a lake.
there in the shallows of a different massacre
my great grandmother gave her name
to your butchertongues. a woman beneath
a larger woman's pale torchlight. and now
don't i sit between these two sweet
poisonous mouths? spent forty years
in the desert confusing your countries
for covenants, though in truth
i am neither convert nor congregant.
a citizen not of one continent.
a colonizer, then. twice over.
when you say G-d you mean
G-vernment. you mean Gr-und

stolen and then stolen.
but no named land will grow
my brand of brier, so now i belong
to both culprit and casualty.
now i'm blessed
with two shadows, their hands
dipped in empire. pardon me
are these both nations?
i don't believe i asked.
not even for one.

this is what you might call a miracle:
G-d cut through the world's belly
to drive our people into it
the angel of death hovering above us as
we left our enemies behind
how did we outrun the salt but
hold this steady march
through the eye of death's needle
there's always another villain.
more pain. more crimson passing through
our doors, framed with lamb's blood
a carnal ribbon of tongues
that was the night we became
so many different deaths. don't ask
why G-d has done this. G-d didn't split
open like a wound. G-d never
condemned innocents to die
diaspora was not a force of nature. it was human
violence, and as long as we live in it
we will never know true liberation

SEA

first there was an ocean, and then a path
to walk our long history across
like a road for the chosen. this story is about
a means of survival. we escaped
drowning in so many floods. ask
not the reason for the salt.
the only route to life will lead
across river after river. luckily
we heard you can heal pain with
water. so one night we soaked our feet
in order to evade
a bright phalanx of raving
murderers. now we fit safely between
the pages of your holy books
every place we've called home
abolished the ocean. we did that
because it was deemed holy.
we built a nation from this saltwater and
we will continue to hold back the tide
even if it comes crashing to our feet

SITTING SHIVA

1.

she left us with plenty of warning. it was always
                wanting

her trick: finding someone new to love. now, a home dim
                           leave

with candlelight. mirrors covered to hide our feast.
                                      fast

the allure of absence. the heart growing towards emptiness.
                                grieving

2.

i spend seven days with my head bowed, weeping
                                swiping

for a stronger prayer. the phone hums at my thigh, pulse
      stranger

quick against the mourning. my palm becomes a window
                morning   widow

of possibility. if i keep watching, a new face presents itself.
                                      fear

3.

don't lecture me on loneliness. i studied loss
                    longing

under the greatest teacher and found its seam with love.
                                        lust

she told me often of the train, how far we should be willing

to travel for death. how this country tugs our family across it.
                desire

4.

i'm most drawn to you when you are gone. imagine my grief
                                      guilt

knowing worry persists. what i wouldn't do for your name
      want

to appear in the bright square in my hand. the single

-mindedness of a steam engine. so close i want it to kiss me.
                                                        kill

5.
you're not dead. you're just not here.

you're in California, where lines are buried.
                           lives   blurred

a flood. a famine. tragedy can bring you closer
                                          closure

if you let it. the world can pull you elsewhere, and it will.

6.
whether a continent placed itself between us or we placed it there

ourselves, the truth is: i went to California to be with you.
                         she   him

we should always be ready to accept love, even if it means living
                                                            leaving

just prove a point, but i've never been that bold.

7.
i like to think she'd understand. she was, if nothing else

a romantic. a dreamer and a journeyer in equal measure.

how else to mourn? i tear my clothes i light the candles.
                     tear my clothes. light the candles.

i say the words and only exit when someone calls me to them.
  say the words   exist

53

TRADESCANTIA

from the mundane root. an oyster plant.
a spiderwort. its variegated purple across
nearly every flowering inch of the world.
sweet Moses-in-the-cradle-lily. amethyst
Angel of Doubt. o Lucy, Saint of Sight,
blind me to etymology, the perse plum pit
in every story about G-d. what wildflower
deserves this wandering? to be buried in
a grave so violet? a name so violent
it once curbed the crucifixion. yes, cursed
to roam until Christ returns. sisyphean
in our ignorance. my aunt gave cuttings
away each winter as a Hanukkah gift
(we all need a little Jew in our lives)
terracotta exodus. tangles of it end-
lessly growing. creeping across oceans.
spreading over continents. the lurking
of a lesser theology. o Lord, leave us
to our legs, our purple leaves. Lord,
where we grow, so do the conditions
for surrender. look us in the root. o Lord,
Lord, let even the seed of a curse bloom
into a blessing.

MATRYOSHKA

when i was very young, i remember asking my mother to show me the long scar across her abdomen. *that's how your brother was born*, she said. my mother was split open by doctors, and out came a son or so i was told. it was very confusing. the only mother i knew who could snap in half so cleanly was a toy - a matryoshka, the Russian meaning "little mother." a set lived on the mantle above the fireplace. my aunt brought the dolls back from the motherland. they stacked so pleasantly together, a row of increasingly tiny figures, and all mothers. i was mesmerized by their unfolding – i'd take the largest, plump, rosy-cheeked mother in my hands and twist, and suddenly out came a small forgery. and then, another mother and another. this chain of breaking open continued. each doll split until i had mothered an entire lineage. was this what the scar meant? my brother, a cut? mothers say when your first is a cesarean birth, your next must be as well. my mother disagreed, so i was born without a surgeon. she was left unsplit, final mother in the set, slight and stubborn, the gall, to give birth to two sons. mother at the end of a severed river. the dolls opened, i lined the mothers up along the mantle like a family reunion. such violent motherhood, to look back and see the hollowed-out shells that mothers made for me. so is it over now? the long act of mothering children to watch them cleave in two? mother who is unbreakable. smallest, irreducible mother, formed to fit inside her own splintering. mother, the thinnest bolt of lightning. mother the head and tail, mother to both. the last mother left alive but how mother becomes mother
mother
mother
mother
broken mother rebuilt. wooden mother. central to each mother: tender fracture mothers make. memory unfolds a mother. time is horizontal, an arrangement of mothers on the mantle. A happening which mothers every happening before it and every mother that follows. now i begin the careful act of re-mothering, fitting the broken dolls around themselves. each mother deliberate in her precise container, which is itself a mother. nothing is displaced or excessive. how clever of motherhood, to be displayed in a single line before it is reshelved. mothers live on a continuum. this is how it works: my wound becomes my mother's wound, and in return her past becomes my story. my scar. my mother texts *i love you like a potato loves the ground* (an old saying from the motherland.) admittedly, i'm lost in a dead language's idioms, but i take it to mean motherhood buries itself deep in the dirt of me. i let it grow there, hiding at my core. mother, i'm frightened. i don't have your grace or your gratitude. i can't hold so much. mother, i envy your ability to be so close to me without being me. i wish i could do that. mother, i can't open and stay whole, can't give and keep a piece of myself. when i try to define motherhood, it breaks and emerges from its own belly more concentrated and exquisite. i become a mother, and why not? can't i snap into a song? can't i open and reveal a smaller, sharper secret? the mother at my center. finally they all rest, the illusion of time dispelled. the world we inherit from our mothers is the same one we borrow from our children.

MAKOT MITZRAYIM

in the voice of Aaron, brother of Moses

i.

i know blood well. it seeps from the walls
here, rivers of it running down our backs
in the sun. brother, i admit that i was skeptical
at first, but i could not deny
my own blood. your name means
drawn from the water and just like that
i watched the Nile bloom red. now Pharaoh
can see it: our blood in his river.

ii.

poor Moses. your stutter and lisp,
your stammer and croak. your weighty tongue.
what irony - that you have been chosen
to speak for us when you can barely speak
for yourself. i know the Lord's rumble
in my throat, brother, loud as the roar
of a bullfrog. let me stand at your side.
make me the voice of
the voice of G-d.

iii.

Moses, birthing a nation is a messy
business, and the woman you call mother
never dirtied herself with your hatching.
what does she know of lineage?
of the flies circling our father's grave?
as a child, ima would pick nits from my scalp
like fat jewels, whisper the names
of the ancestors who died to bring us here.

iv.
you say there will be ten in total
if His commands are not obeyed.
i wish it hadn't come to this
but you cannot tame a god, brother.
every beast devours what's beneath Him.
only He can leash Himself.

v.
i admit, some miracles
are difficult to stomach.
first the grain withers to blight,
then the cattle drop one by one
dead as the stones we use to build
statues of their dead. it's the smell.
the curdle of livestock. the rot
of fields and fields.

vi.
when i look upon
their disfigured bodies, red welts
cankered and caked in sun,
it helps to imagine Egypt
as a blister to be lanced
from the earth. i force myself
to remember righteousness.
that's what gets me through the day.
but you. how do you stand it, brother?
i only announce the coming of the sword
but you're the one who swings it.

vii.
what terrible destruction. what
burning and thunder. Exodus is nothing

but a rancid dream. while
my brothers are killed, my brother's
G-d kills every day. oh Lord,
what curse you have given him
and cursed me in turn?

viii.
Moses, do you remember
our mother. you were a child once
buoyed by a river. i watched
it carry you far away
but not this far.

ix.
the blood should have been enough.
brother, you must know how
to end this without slaughter.

ix.
i've heard what comes next:
the thin door that separates
me from the Angel of Death.
Lord, don't you know which brother i am?

ix.
i won't speak the next plague
into being. i won't claim your religion
if this is what you expect
of your priests.

ix.
Moses, do you understand now?
what is the cost
of birthing a nation?
how many miracles

does the work require?
if one god threatens to kill you
for praying to another
then at which altar
should you worship?

FIFTH DRINK

when

i offer

to

be the designated

driver

i

do it for me.

WHAT WE'RE OWED

"If you cannot endure the bad, you will not live to witness the good."

Yiddish proverb

so say the zaydes. so say
the aunts who endured those
who endured death. the hierarchy
of distance, of who's been closest
to the gun barrel and lived.
they say our life lacks steel.
lacks broken glass and riots
with sinister roots. little
do they know what grows
rotten at the center of this country.
untamable knot. to witness good
is not necessarily to partake in it.

THE DISCOVERY OF DEATH

imagine it like this: two brothers. one
offers the Lord the harvest of his field,
a bounty. but instead the younger son
presents a lamb. G-d turns away the yield
of crops for meat, so then the first of first
-borns murderously strikes his brother down
in jealousy and afterwards is cursed
to roam the Earth. and although much is known
of Cain, it's Abel – poised to sacrifice
another breathing body – he's the boy
who doesn't get his due. he knew the price
of flesh is greater than the price of soil.
and so death was perfected by the eldest
brother but discovered by the youngest.

TETRAGRAMMATON

I.

my mother always sang the harmonies
in synagogue, and her voice was
like no instrument. magic enough to cast
a shatter on my siddur. on my understanding.
four intervals of majesty. my childhood
wrecked with wonder. the not-knowing
made a temple of that temple.
i traced the Hebrew with my English tongue
and hoped i was pronouncing prayers correctly.
i sang when it was asked of me, stayed
silent when it counted. would watch
the old men rocking back and forth
as if they knew the will of G-d, whatever
mystery hid beneath the black keys on a piano.
astonished by the words i wouldn't say
aloud. by the world i couldn't conceive.

II.

all i knew was sound. i learned the arc
of letters, their gravel in my throat.
missing vowels hidden in the script
but somehow known. was i expected
to understand or just to sing? melody,
my only heritage. i couldn't find the line
from then to now. and finally, that name.
the single word. the theonym i wasn't
meant to speak. why not?
if voice is what lifts a word from the page,
unfastens it from death and reveals
its meaning, then what am i to make
of names that shed their sound in air?
i had a voice without a history to bind it.
and so the letters ran together. blended
ink. no words held court in me - just song.

III.

the more i grew, the more it seemed to me
that parts of faith were kept opaque. one day
i witnessed a prayer trip over its own history
on the way to G-d. so what? i thought
at first. i always knew the truth. i'm a poet.
even my awe is performative. but it stuck
in me like a thorn. like a nail. i pulled it out
and became it, fancied myself so sharp
you couldn't even see the edge of me.
invisible right up until the moment
i cut the air beneath a rabbi's sermon.
soft underbelly of a synagogue. yes,
i abandoned mystery for a more earthly
ignorance, resigned to dry disdain for men
who dangled G-d in front of me like a fish
hook. i didn't speak for fear i'd break my tongue.

IV.

i nicked my face with the blade
of Occam's Razor, bled a spec of red
onto the sanctuary floor. then, like a flood
that brings the end of doubt, i was destroyed
by a single note, a long lost skeleton
key ungating a deadbolt. i'm open now.
i make room for grace, empty for it.
content to know what i don't know,
i clear the table and wait to be amazed.
i don't believe in G-d. i believe in sound.
the not-knowing. no language, art, or science
here. no bird calls. no church band. no orchestra
of wayward mothers. only a skybound tremble
made magic. the promise and the payoff.
a word is not a map to G-d, but it can show
you where to look. it can tell you what to sing.

LISTEN, THE GHOSTS OUT IN THE OLD COUNTRY CAN'T LIGHT CANDLES

after Diane Seuss

Shabbas is a holy day. once
the sun is down, the striking of matches is forbidden.
out in the old country, ghosts unsettle the waters
and step onto dry land like a phantom congregation

called to prayer. listen, Shabbas is a day of rest
and though the ghosts are not at rest, they still follow
the old country's laws, so the houses stay dark.
the ghosts are heavy with jewels and history,

old bubbes bent low with river water.
they lived out in the old country before
it was old. before it was a country. ghosts
know all about borders, how your synagogue can be

on one side when the sun goes down
and the next morning your language is a crime.
but they were always a people of compromise.
when Rabbi Rashi and Rabbeinu Tam couldn't decide

how the mezuzah would hang on a door frame
they split the difference and affixed it
at a 45 degree angle. when the Polish or the Russians
burned their houses, they moved to their own

walled-in neighborhoods. they made it seem
like their idea. they all toppled each other. the Jews
the Romanovs, the Communists. they liked to play
a game. they called it Russian roulette

and no one knew when it would be their turn
in the chamber. listen, if you see one of them

all you need to do is open a book. in death
they gravitate towards familiar scents: wet ink.

the taut air between what a word means
and what it can do when you set it on fire.
they lived on the banks of the wrong river. crossed
the wrong border. and after all, a border is just

an imaginary river cutting through the earth.
but the ghosts out in the old country can't hurt you.
they can't turn on any of your lights. they can only
ever see by the glow of a match if someone else

strikes it. the day you die is a holy day, so for them
it is always Shabbas. for them, the old laws are still the laws.
for them your house is closed unless they see
a mezuzah on its door. unless it is affixed correctly.

THE OTHER MOSES

my mother knows that to make the world new, you must first remove
the old. she taught me that to create something, you have to break
something in half. destruction begets wonders. that's why all the
         prophets
get swallowed or burned. she bore my brother via C-section, bore the
         razor
as it cut him out. from her childhood apartment, you can follow
Hunts Point until it becomes Southern. bear right where the road

splits at Freeman, go a few blocks north and you'll see it: a road
dividing the city in two. the Cross Bronx Expressway was meant to
         move
people through the neighborhood, but it left the neighborhood fallow
instead. pushed folks out. an asphalt Exodus. the whole borough
         broke
open like an old testament ocean, all thanks to a single man who
         praised
the god of capital and worshiped only at the altar of profit

margins: Robert Moses, a cynical prophet
of highways and headlights who spent decades eroding
the city from the inside out. Moses once said "i raise
my stein to the builder who can remove ghettos without moving
people as i hail the chef who can make omelets without breaking
eggs." what hubris, though i suppose he was just following

G-d's example. division as creation. first, there's nothing. what
         follows
is separation - light from darkness. earth from sky. prophets
from heretics. it's the same thing my mother taught me: to break
the old world in favor of a new one. in the beginning, G-d rode
that narrow divide between the ocean and the land, moved
rivers and toppled mountains. that's what Moses did: raze

houses to the ground so he might one day raise
the housing prices. in 1955 my mother's family followed
a trail of her people across the East River and moved
to Queens. see, for Moses, anyone who stood in the way of profit
had to be cut out. he replaced their homes with roads,
their congregation songs with the squeal of brakes.

i think he wanted what many Jewish men want: to break
into the Temple of Whiteness and then be praised
as its savior, and like many of them, he saw destruction on the road
to deliverance. Moses wished for power and wound up at Pharaoh's
table. in the end, he wasn't a prophet. he was a war profiteer
with different weapons. he proved that no scripture can move

the wheel of history, so now i follow my mother's faith. i move
through the world like a scalpel, raise my blade to this bad prophet.
break the power broker. the Other Moses. his long and costly road.

MY SHADOW AND THE BOTTLE

after Jaz Sufi

i. dusk

a riddle i can't answer:
i have a shadow and a bottle.
one of them follows me everywhere and the other
looks like my father if i squint hard enough
but which is which? each morning
i think i can tell them apart.
the shadow. the bottle.
but once the sun goes down
everything becomes its own shadow.
my hands are my father's hands.
if you practice something enough times
it becomes an unshakable part of you.
the half of you turned away from the light.
in this way maybe my shadow is just another addiction.
i give it nicknames so i won't be as frightened each night:
partner in wine. unwavering brother.
honeyed assassin dogging my steps.
what do i do with this bottle i can't get rid of?
i can't go into it
and come back out unchanged.
i can build a ship inside it,
but it won't take me anywhere worth going.
so i kill the bottle and true,
that is a kind of death. but if this is about
one thing i've learned from my father
it's that you can't escape your own shadow,
a thing that is tethered to you by blood
and the absence of light. after all
if this ends the same way it began
then death will greet me with a bottle
and a face like my father's.

luckily, my people do not believe in resurrections.
when you leave, you stay gone,
and i do
but whether or not i decide to live
i will still have a shadow.

—

ii. dawn

i will still have a shadow
whether or not i decide to live
and i do
when you leave, you stay gone.
my people do not believe in resurrections,
but if i'm lucky, i will greet death
as i have faced my father's bottles.
if this ends the same way it began,
it's that. it's tethered to the light,
the absence of blood. after all
i can't escape my own shadow.
it is the one thing i've learned from my father
but this is not about that kind of death
true, the bottle kills, so
i don't take it. anywhere worth going
can be built like a ship.
i can't go inside a bottle
and come back out unchanged.
so what do i do with this bottle i can't get rid of?
a honeyed assassin dogging my steps
unwavering brother. partner in wine.
i give it nicknames so i won't be as frightened.
each night, my addiction is just another shadow.
the half of me turned away from the light.
that unshakable part of me. but i have practiced,

have held my father's hands in my hands
enough times to know
that everything undoes its own shadow
once the sun comes up.
the shadow. the bottle.
i think i can tell them apart.
which is which. each morning
looks like my father if i squint hard enough.
one of them follows me everywhere and the other
is a bottle. is a shadow. is
a riddle i've answered.

NEXT YEAR IN JERUSALEM

When we sing the prayer after the meal
we use the melody I learned
in childhood. That way I won't get lost
in the dead language. The wrong legends.
Old keys to a new map. Where is Jerusalem
today, and where will it be next year?
If I cannot hold my mother's hand tonight
then am I part of the diaspora?
If I cannot welcome my father
into my home, then do I live in exile?
Home is where the hurt stops.
Where the army halts. Unweaponed.
Edgeless as my grandmother's
many-scripted tongue. We've never been
but we're always on our way.
Only the road that once led there
is a border now. A wall. A window
I look through to see the nation
of your faces. So wherever we raise
a glass of wine across a table
that is where I'm from. Where
I'm going. There will be enough
Jerusalem there in the late-summer
mint. Jerusalem, a door I unlock
with the key you hid in the hollow
stone. Holy city of my mother's laugh
as it Jerusalems the dining room.
Home, the place you leave
to find. The place you leave
blood to avoid bloodshed.
Next year we'll be together there.
I promise there's no place like it.

button
poetry

NOTES

Ninth Plague
The initial draft of this poem was written in August 2017, after the Unite the Right rally in Charlottesville, VA on 8/11/17, the subsequent protest in Durham, NC on 8/14/17 during which protestors toppled a monument of a confederate soldier, the solar eclipse on 8/21/17, and a march to end white supremacy in Berkeley, CA on 8/27/17. The italicized text comes from Eduardo C. Corral's poem "Testaments Scratched into a Water Station Barrel."

Punnett Square for the Ways I Die
A Punnett Square is a square diagram used by biologists to predict the probability of specific genotypes in a cross or breeding experiment given known data about both parents. It is named after Reginald C. Punnett.

Leil Shimurim
"Leil Shimurim" (לֵיל שִׁמֻּרִים) translates roughly into "night of vigils" or "night that is guarded" and refers to the first two nights of Passover.

ELEVEN
This poem is written after Patricia Smith's poem "13 Ways of Looking at 13" which is itself after Wallace Stevens' poem "Thirteen Ways of Looking at a Blackbird." The phrase "living truthfully under imaginary circumstances" is attributed to Sanford Meisner and was how he described acting. Biblical Hebrew uses diacritical marks (or cantillation) to instruct a reader on the melody of a passage.

J.I.N.O. (Jew In Name Only)
"J.I.N.O." is a term invented by conservative political commentator Ben Shapiro. He uses it to derogatorily refer to American Jews who he feels are not expressing or living into Jewish identity in ways that align with certain right-wing and/or Zionist beliefs. This poem is

written after the Angel Nafis and Jon Sands poem "Black Girl White Boy" which is itself after Terrance Hayes's poem "The Blue Seuss."

The Plane Lands at Ben Gurion and Every Passenger Bursts Into Song
Often, passengers arriving in Jerusalem via plane will sing "Hatikvah," the Israeli national anthem, upon landing. The "Bass" text of this poem is composed from an erasure of the English translation of "Hatikvah." "Hatikvah" is also the primary instrumental sample used in Anderson .Paak's song "Come Down."

NUREMBERG LAWS
The Citizenship Law of 1935 and the Law for the Protection of German Blood and German Honor of 1935 were two acts passed by the Nazi government, collectively known as the Nuremberg Laws. Part II of this poem (LAWS) is an erasure of the translated text of the Nuremberg Laws. Part IV (NUMBERS) is an anagram-sonnet in which each line only consists of the 13 letters within the term "NUREMBERG LAWS."

Birthright
Taglit-Birthright Israel is a program that provides free trips to Israel-Palestine for young Jewish Americans with the goal of deepening their ties to the land and country. Birthright has been widely criticized for serving as a form of Zionist indoctrination and propaganda for American Jews.

My Depression Explains Me to My Mother
This poem is written after a loose series of "My Depression" poems: Sabrina Benaim's poem "Explaining My Depression to My Mother" and RJ Walker's poem "My Mother Explains My Depression to Me."

Twice-Contained
On December 11, 2019, President Trump signed the "Executive Order Combating Anti-Semitism" which directed the Department of Education to protect Jewish students under Title VI of the Civil

Rights Act, the implication being that Judaism should be protected as a 'race' or 'national origin' per the law's text. The implications were that the DOE would enforce the new order to pressure institutions into suppressing pro-Palestinian speech and action on campus, and second, that American Jews being regarded as a separate 'nation,' plays on antisemitic tropes of dual-loyalty and raises the specter of the Nuremberg Laws.

Sitting Shiva
Shiva or שבעה (literally "seven") is a Jewish mourning practice during which immediate family members of the deceased remain in the home for seven days following a burial.

tradescantia
Tradescantia is a houseplant which blooms purple. It's common name, "Wandering Jew," originates from the Christian antisemitic myth of the Wandering Jew, who, after taunting Jesus on the way to his crucifixion, is cursed to wander the earth until the second coming.

Matryoshka
Admittedly, the conceit of this poem is based on a slight mistranslation. The Russian word Matryoshka (матрёшка) is more accurately translated as "little matron." However, the history and cultural meaning of the doll itself is widely associated with motherhood.

Makot Mitzrayim
"Makot Mitzrayim" (מכות מצרים) is the Hebrew term for the ten plagues of Egypt. According to the Bible, Moses spoke with a speech impediment, so his brother Aaron served as his primary communicator. Aaron also later became the high priest of the Hebrews.

Tetragrammaton
The Tetragrammaton refers to the four-letter Hebrew name for G-d, which is never spoken aloud.

listen, the ghosts out in the old country can't light candles
This poem is written after Diane Seuss's poem "People, the ghosts down in North-of-the-South aren't see-through."

The Other Moses
Robert Moses was an urban planner and public administrator who heavily influenced the growth and development of New York City throughout the mid-20th century. He is responsible for the construction of what was at the time the most expensive mile of road ever built: a segment of the Cross Bronx Expressway, and his policies and projects displaced thousands of primarily non-white residents. Although he was born to Jewish parents, Moses later converted to Christianity.

My Shadow & the Bottle
This poem is written after Jaz Sufi's poem "My Mother and the Bottle" which is itself after Warsan Shire's poem "Backwards."

Next Year in Jerusalem
Traditionally, "next year in Jerusalem" is the last phrase spoken at a Passover seder. For many years, it was understood as the aspirational return of the Jewish people to Jerusalem. Contemporary meanings and uses differ in how they regard the position of the Jewish people in Israel-Palestine vis-à-vis the diaspora and what it means to have a "home."

ACKNOWLEDGMENTS

Thank you to the readers and editors of the publications where many of these poems first appeared:

AGNI: "Red Sea"

ANMLY: "The Plane Lands at Ben Gurion and Every Passenger Bursts Into Song"; "Matryoshka"; "tradescantia"

Button Poetry (Youtube): "Birthright"; "Red Sea" (video); "My Shadow & the Bottle"; the Drink sequence (as "Blackout" video); "Incantation" (video)

Knight's Library: The Drink sequence (as "Blackout")

The Laurel Review: "NUREMBERG LAWS"

New South: "Ninth Plague"

PANK: "UMBER" (from NUREMBERG LAWS, as "The _____ Question.")

Pleiades: "From Here"; "Barbra's Nose"

The Shmita Project: "listen, the ghosts out in the old country can't light candles"; "Next Year in Jerusalem"

RHINO Poetry: "wine/water/blood"

Washington Square Review: "Punnett Square for the Ways I Die"

An earlier draft of "Tetragrammaton" appears in *Word! The Loft @ 50 Chapbook*.

"Incantation" and "Everything I Want to Hear" appear in the chapbook *XV* (Nomadic Press/Black Lawrence, 2020)

This book was completed with generous funding and assistance from Rimon: The Minnesota Jewish Arts Council. This book was also made possible by the voters of Minnesota through a grant from the Metropolitan Regional Arts Council (MRAC), thanks to a legislative appropriation from the arts and cultural heritage fund.

Thank you, Sam, Tanesha, Spencer, Riley, Patrick, Charley, and everyone at Button Poetry who trusted this work and gave me the opportunity to share it.

Thank you, Andrea Gibson, for selecting and believing in this collection.

Thank you, Michael Mlekoday for your time, attention, and thoughtfulness in handling these poems. Gratitude to Julia Kolchinksy Dasbach and Jay Ward for your kind and gracious words.

I am indebted to my Jewish friends and family who were an integral part of this process: Alex Baskin, Estelle Cohen, Susan Cohen, Gaily Ezer, Peter Goldberg, Em Podhorcer, Seth Rose, Mike Rosen, Dan Samorodnitsky, Josh Smith, Andrew Stelzer, Marsha Toma.

Thank you to the writers and readers who helped shape this work, knowingly or otherwise: Abe Becker, Anna Binkovitz, Mary Kay Delaney, Collin Edmonds, Reggie Edmonds, José Gonzalez, Natalie Kaplan, Em Kianka, Tanesha Nicole Kozler, Victoria Morgan, sam sax, Ollie Schminkey, Javi Somejo, Jaz Sufi, and Anna Šverclová.

Endless gratitude to the communities that have taught me, seen me, and celebrated me: West Club, DYWC, C4, the Dopenhagen, WeSLAM, 142 Cross, Mango House, the Noodles/Spatzle, Oxbow, the Muse, Berkeley Slam, Boneshaker Books, BuckSlam, The Loft – all the artists, organizers, and community members who gave me a home. The list keeps growing. You have raised and continue to raise me.

Susan, Peter, Ross, Jess, Evan, Iris: What can I say? Thank you for being my family. Love you all.

Mel: Thank you for helping me see both the forest and the trees. For everything.

ABOUT THE AUTHOR

Zach Goldberg is a writer, educator, and arts administrator from Durham, NC. He is the author of the chapbook *XV* (Nomadic Press/Black Lawrence) and the winner of the 2021 Button Poetry Chapbook Contest. Zach is a former member of the 2018 and 2019 Berkeley Slam Team and is a proud co-founder of BuckSlam MN. His work has appeared in journals including *AGNI*, *Pleiades*, and *RHINO*. He lives on occupied Dakota land in Minneapolis, MN. Find him online @gach_zoldberg.

AUTHOR BOOK RECOMMENDATIONS

Birthright By George Abraham

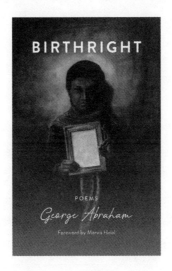

Birthright is as inventive as it is tender, a collection unlike any other bursting with brilliant forms and surprising language. This book is truly a map, a cartography of human spirit. Inside, you'll find an atlas containing both suffering and resolve in equal measure, seamlessly blending personal and political into something greater. Abraham writes, "teach me to love / a country without unmothering another" and yes, we are the children of history, which is just as messy as it is gorgeous.

Composition By Junious "Jay" Ward

COMPOSITION

JUNIOUS WARD

Unending praise for Jay Ward's *Composition*, which leaves nothing unsaid and pulls no punches. In this provocative and challenging collection, Ward unearths a dense world beneath our very feet. Careful navigating these pages or you might cut yourself on this sharp, insightful craft. Don't look away – what you find will demand (and deserve) your attention.

Even The Saints Audition By Raych Jackson

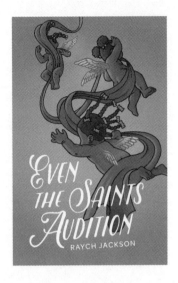

Yes, *Even The Saints Audition* is a sermon, but not the kind you might be expecting. In these pages, Raych Jackson asks us to consider the tension between a child in the pews and a preacher at the pulpit. She waxes poetic with the grace that only a sinner can muster in a collection that is equal parts coming-of-age and coming-to-Jesus. Of course, prophets aren't always as perfect as we make them out to be...

OTHER BOOKS BY BUTTON POETRY

If you enjoyed this book, please consider checking out some of our others, below. Readers like you allow us to keep broadcasting and publishing. Thank you!

Kevin Kantor, *Please Come Off-Book*
Ollie Schminkey, *Dead Dad Jokes*
Reagan Myers, *Afterwards*
L.E. Bowman, *What I Learned From the Trees*
Patrick Roche, *A Socially Acceptable Breakdown*
Rachel Wiley, *Revenge Body*
Ebony Stewart, *BloodFresh*
Ebony Stewart, *Home.Girl.Hood.*
Kyle Tran Myhre, *Not A Lot of Reasons to Sing, but Enough*
Steven Willis, *A Peculiar People*
Topaz Winters, *So, Stranger*
Darius Simpson, *Never Catch Me*
Blythe Baird, *Sweet, Young, & Worried*
Siaara Freeman, *Urbanshee*
Robert Wood Lynn, *How to Maintain Eye Contact*
Junious 'Jay' Ward, *Composition*
Usman Hameedi, *Staying Right Here*
Sean Patrick Mulroy, *Hated for the Gods*
Sierra DeMulder, *Ephemera*
Taylor Mali, *Poetry By Chance*
Matt Coonan, *Toy Gun*
Matt Mason, *Rock Stars*
Miya Coleman, *Cottonmouth*
Ty Chapman, *Tartarus*
Lara Coley, *ex traction*
DeShara Suggs-Joe, *If My Flowers Bloom*
Ollie Schminkey, *Where I Dry the Flowers*
Edythe Rodriguez, *We, the Spirits*
Topaz Winters, *Portrait of my Body as a Crime I'm Still Committing*

Available at *buttonpoetry.com/shop* and more!

BUTTON BEST SELLERS

Neil Hilborn, *Our Numbered Days*
Hanif Abdurraqib, *The Crown Ain't Worth Much*
Olivia Gatwood, *New American Best Friend*
Sabrina Benaim, *Depression & Other Magic Tricks*
Melissa Lozada-Oliva, *peluda*
Rudy Francisco, *Helium*
Rachel Wiley, *Nothing Is Okay*
Neil Hilborn, *The Future*
Phil Kaye, *Date & Time*
Andrea Gibson, *Lord of the Butterflies*
Blythe Baird, *If My Body Could Speak*
Rudy Francisco, *I'll Fly Away*
Andrea Gibson, *You Better Be Lightning*
Rudy Francisco, *Excuse Me As I Kiss The Sky*

Available at *buttonpoetry.com/shop* and more!